AF579444

Acknowledgments

This book wouldn't have been possible if it wasn't for Asad helping me out on this project. I learnt so much from him whenever we were together working, discussions and agreements, discussing about life, death and a lot of other philosophical concepts. It was a bumpy ride but we made it and "The Agony" came into making.

Thank you so much, Asad Khawar.

www.asadkhawar.com

INDEX

INDEX

Introduction

I am an inhabitant, abandoned on this wrecked planet of thoughts. An island with a palm tree, a long-lost wanderer. It is difficult for me to introduce myself because I myself am also trying to find my real self. All I can tell is that I'm 17 and my whole life, all I've known is suffering and failure so to be heard and seen I started pouring myself down on these pieces of paper, in the form of words, and those words started to form the shape of poems.

What am I?

I am all the hate I was served with,
all the bullies I have dealt with,
all the failures I have faced,
I am all the opportunities I have chased.

I am all the bridges I have burned,
all the paths I have turned,
all the hopes devastated,
I am all the love i invested,

I am all the grief I carried,
all the dreams I buried,
all the tears I have shed,
I am the one with existential dread.

2
Curse

My veins are popped up,
My brain is messed up,
My heart is stained,
My soul is in pain.

These are my last breathes,
This grief had me having a heavy
chest,
Unlike a young bird in the nest,
I cant fly and I'll die in this bed.

I won't make it till tomorrow,
I'll be dead by midnight,
Haunted By my sorrows,
Demons asking for a fight.

I'm in a battlefield,
Battling my thoughts,
Neither i have a shield,
Nor I have a sword.

These shocks before death,
These thoughts before death,
Making my situation worse,
Life is nothing more than a curse.

3

Rusted world

My world was rusting,
eating itself up,
tearing and falling,
I tried to pour up a cup,
Skies turning black,
where I sat in the field,
Who was there? who I saw? who he see?
It was all going black,
what a sight to see,
They move to me so silently,
but why do they walk past me?
Can you take me?
I asked frighteningly,
I should sit,
I should stay they said stridently,
When will you take me?
when will you hold me?
After four, after five, maybe three.

4

Misconception

This relation with death as if it is my only friend,
It is misunderstood as if it is the end.

It is the fire that does not consumes the wood,
No one can escape it no matter how hard they try.

Death is not insane, it is end of the pain,
A route changed not just switching lane.

This world is just a pool, people will tell you to swim and watch you as you sunk,

A desert where you will be kept down and people will watch you as you shrunk.

You will be lit on fire and your ashes will be set free in the air,
They will all watch because none of them care.

You will suffocate and they'll steal your oxygen,
They will pollute you with their lies and it will be just an origin.

You will become thirsty and they will steal your water,
You will sweat more as the weather turns hotter.

Now my friend, is death really an end?
Maybe not you, but it is my real friend.

5
House of God

house of god stabbed and penetrated,
it's strands sliced and separated,
cased in his own hands decorated,
the scars it had, never faded,
same condition, never recuperated,
he was living speculated,
they built a plot and confederated,
completely destroyed and devastated,
where he went wrong, he contemplated,
tired of telling truth but they still negate,
where will he find peace? someone navigate,
maybe not, he don't want help no more,
his knees are bruised from falling on the floor,
he will walk, injured, in the streets, won't knock any door,
will float in the ocean, will stay offshore,
he will live in the past, his heart won't restore,
stuck in life, like a bullet in the bore,
he will, but he don't want to live anymore,
merrily he will carry the house of god,
will bow to no one except the only lord.

6
Sins Payment

There are no rewinds,
And no one here reminds,
It was all cool what we had,
Now all is gone and I'm sad.

Promised you I'll stay out of reach,
Can't tolerate, memories still bothers me,
I want to let go of your memories and you,
But I can't help it because I keep on coming back to you.

Can't remember everything its been a while,
I'm coming for you even if I've to cross Nile,
Every now and then I chase you,
But I'm scared too much to face you.

You wasted our bond and I'm faceless,
I'll fix everything, can't wait no patience,
Either this will be the new start or I'll end up in Sahara,
A fresh good morning or last sayonara.

E.N.D

He was in the dark wishing for an end,
Trying to escape next door,
With a book in hand and a flower in hair,
With no successor and no heir,
With heart crushed and eyes full of despair,
Trapped in his own mind,
A flesh, bone, armor that was once too kind,
Is scared of everyone and hides behind,
No wonder how the thoughts turned inside,
Went from wishing to commit suicide,
Caged in cemented walls beneath the falls,
Towards the doors of end slowly he crawls.

8

Where are you?

I'm trying to find you,
I'm looking for you,
In every petal,
In earth's breath,
In every sea,
In every depth,
In the dawn,
In the dusk,
In the water,
In the musk,
In the leaves grown,
In the seeds bowed,
Over the hills,
In daffodils,
In the sky,
On the clouds,
On the dust,
On the ground,
In the night,
In the day,
Every night,
Every day.

I don`t know if i have made god
my muse or my muse my god.

Fading Wishes

I have been wishing death for a long now,
Yet I'm still alive somehow,
I died when I was sixteen,
Won't be buried until I'm seventy.

It is the natural rule that world will always be cruel,
Not everyone drowns and not everyone floats in this pool,
Not everyone fails and not everyone passes in this school,
Used to believe in people, what a fool.

Between this all I made friends with the grim reaper,
He used to chew on people as if they were a teether,
Used to have a scythe and use to cut souls as they were crops, What a fire breather.

Lies Lies Lies

Setting fire to the rain,
My spirit admires this pain,
Shedding these crocodile tears,
Nothing is faker than the smile that I wear.

Had a lot going through my mind,
But it is fine it is not the first time,
People I know as my family are the first to doubt me,
They are spreading rumors who barely know about me.

Caught up in this world full of lies,
I don't know if I'll survive another night,
I am not broken, broken hearts are in two,
My parts are so far apart they can't renew.

Insomniac

Caged in the jail of misery, having heart attacks,
Post-traumatic stress is making me an insomniac,
Having this weight on my chest as heavy as a potato sack.

It is difficult to survive this night,
In a tunnel and can't seem to find some light,
I was trying to build myself but I lost trace to the site.

I guess I'll be dead by dawn,
Don't cry over me don't moan,
When I was alive, I was all alone,
Had no one with me not even a clone

12

Night

It is raining every night,
It is stormy, Thunder's lights,
Tears are pouring down my eyes,
Not clear but hazardous skies.

Starting from the lids,
Running down my cheeks,
Staying on my chin,
Dropping on my bed sheets.

My bed is wet by tears,
My pillows knows all my fears,
The voices in my head,
Are making me mad.

13

Morning

Now it's morning,
Heart's still mourning,
Gunfire's in my head,
Wanna die in this bed.

The day is starting,
The sun is rising,
May all these storms and lightning's,
Don't get more frightening.

Afternoon

Sitting all alone,
Throwing away the stones,
Cracks in the bones,
When I'm alone,
I wish you had a clone.

I can't get you out of my head,
Your loving is making me mad,
Your leaving has made me sad,
Was I this much bad?
I am numb, my face is red.

15

Evening

My mind's hollow,
Full of sorrow,
I am here today,
Maybe gone tomorrow,

I'm in my own dump,
Wanna get outta this slump,
In here I feel like,
I'm just a bum,

Devil in my head calls,
Says I should sell my soul,
And I must pay ,
For my sins scrolled.

The setting of the Sun

The sun sets,the light dies,
The moon rises, the night skies,
The truth hides, the white lies,
Cold nights, swelled eyes,
Crowded mind, a bee hive,
Had no sleep, morning, five
Ocean of trust, took a dive,
Outside you, all flee,
On the inside, I bleed,
I may crash, I should not speed,
Not safe, it is armed and dangerous,
It is never calm, always a bit rageous,
Not a coward, always courageous.
Who do I have? who do I call?
Somebody, hold me before I fall,
Someone, answer my yell and call.

Graveyard

I have a graveyard in myself,
Row's finished so started making a shelf,
Dreams stacked over stacks.

I am screaming inside my head,
Where's my god I just need some help,
Give me inner peace or death in this bed.

I don't feel anything I'm numb inside,
It feels I'm dead or fully paralyzed,
Specific thoughts are making me more traumatized.

18

Silence

Restless days,
Sleepless nights,
Meaningless life.
A lone flower,
Surrounded by a bee hive.

Always replaced,
Always misused,
Always mislead.
My soul is bruised,
From core to head.

I am a waste of life,
I broke your heart,
And you buried mine.
I want to go six feet deep in the ground,
Just want to die without any sound.

19

War

Love is war, war is love,
Love is hate, hate is love,
Love is change, change is love,
Love is neglecting, neglecting is love,
Love is a gun, a gun is love,
Love is death, death is love.

20
Falling

I will be happiest the day I die,
It won't be me but somebody will cry,
And that somebody would surely lie.

Was too young to go through such burdens,
Used to put all of my griefs in seven curtains,
Smiled throughout my life while inside I was hurting.

Anxiety used to hit me like a boulder falling off the mountain,
All the voices in my head always kept shouting,
The wolves inside me were always howling.

There's no end to the pain you must be numb,
Things will get unfathomable and you will succumb,
Suicidal thoughts will stick with you like gum.

Success

Unlike rain in the monsoons,
My tears are falling in the noon,
Its all fiction and toons.
Failure pointing at my head like a goon.

I want to run out through the back door,
Was going through elevator to the top floor,
Was in middle of ocean trying to reach the shore,
Maybe I just want to go back home.

This long road to success,
In between it's a complete mess,
This is no game, this is no chess,
Without struggle what is success anyways.

22
Torn Soul

Unstitched scars,
Unhealed soul,
Wounded heart,
Wounded soul,
Bruised knees,
Crooked toes,
Hidden enemies,
A hundred foes,
digging and digging,
shoveling and shoveling,
Faceless city,
faceless king,
No Human came,
not a single ding,
not a single coo coo,
not a cock-a-doodle-doo,
only me, and my god,
Like an owner, and a parrot on rod,
When all are in one third,
The god told me I was heard,
Couldn't sleep, couldn't rest,
He heard me, I felt blessed,
Like a soldier, with a shovel unlike sword,
I cut through the heart of land, and give myself to the lord.

Peace

people in hell and devil on earth,
the day is dark and the night is bright,
dead are alive and the alive are dead,
silence is loud and voice is silent,
eyes are blind and the blind can see,
the kings are poor and the poor are kings,
the kind are dead and the undead, unkind,
the smoke is there, where, there is no fire,
humans are cheap and humanity expensive,
insects on ground and humans in dirt,
meaningless is meaningful, and,
meaningful is meaningless,
love is full of hate, and, hate of loyalty,
friends are foes and foes, friends,
earth is hell and graves heaven,
life is pain and death is peace.

24

Streets

Condition is worse than a drought,
Wanting them tears to come out,
No water, my eyes are dried out.

Darkness all over my room,
Thought you were the reason to live,
Turns out you were my doom.

Saw a straight road but it was a trap,
Angel of death waiting on my doorstep,
Was on the streets of life but lost my map.

I'm lost and I don't know where to go,
No home to stay and no place that I know,
Had one friend he also turned into a foe.

Confused by streets unlike the spiders web,
Wandering in the streets lost and trapped,
Coming out of my place is my only regret.

In love you are either lost or found,
You die with a smile or without any sound,
When dead either you go to heaven or
you're hell bound.

25

Knaves

the dents we have,
the scars,
they were not,
from enemies,
or from people afar,
the deepest ones,
came from people in vicinity,
the ones who were there,
the ones with unity,
we should fear the close,
the dangers they arose,
we think they are kindly,
we better not trust blindly,
they are the first ones,
to dance on our graves,
we better cut them out,
they are all knaves,
better live alone,
better get the throne.

Blown candles

you left me alone, in dark, not a candle in sight,
rushed away, leaving me, alone in the lonely night,
it was raining on me, even before you throw me,
storms, thunders, hazards, were on me,
breaking me down, tearing me apart,
no one to hold me, no one to support,
rocks, stones, pebbles, marbles, concrete,
all were pouring down as leaves falling from trees,
didnt have a place to go, my only home went
away,
my only shine, my only spark, my only sunlight ray,
I thought I could take it, I thought I was brave,
I was wrong, I found myself digging my own grave.

Refusal

when they all burn,
in the fires of hate,
when they are refused,
to go through heaven's gate,
when they all are cursing,
their own fate,
when everyone,
is looking for a mate,
no one will help,
no one will care,
they did not wanted to die,
they loved their life,
they always hated on others,
now they will all walk on a knife,
should have blowed the matches they lit,
to live, they should have died a bit.

28
Sense

when nonsense makes sense,
when people are done being dense,
when mysteries start to reveal,
when heart and mind makes a deal,
when the ship meets the shore,
when they get to know what they didn't knew
before,
when the aircraft finally lands,
when their mindset at the end expands,
when they finally believe,
in the truth they leave,
unheard and unseen,
when they know, what they mean,
when they pull their finger off the trigger,
holding a gun makes their hands shiver,
now apologizing for mistakes they made,
I will forgive but my scars won't fade.

Can`t Run

there's death in life,
and life in death,

can't run from death in life,
can't run from life in death,

run, run, run away,
but where will you run to?
farther you run,
near to death you go,

once you walk in,
you can never walk out,

end your life and you are a coward,
live your life and you dead already,

the stones they throw,
the walls they cast,
the face they show,
then change so fast,

you can't escape,
you can't run,
hide in a cloak,
or run to the sun.

30

Dust

of dust, on dust, from dust, to dust,
maybe dust is the ultimate end,
then human, why so arrogant?

why so full of violence?
why are you so cruel?
can't you just stay silent?

human, why so inhumane?
why do you only give pain?
why do you want to expand your reign?

wonder about the God's just,
the best and the worst,
all rest in the dust,

the fact of which you are unaware,
joys of life are the afterlife's despair,
the way you moving, you will be beyond repair.

31

Diamonds

To the story untold,
To the diamonds unsold,
To the pale enchanted gold,
To the soul that is cold,
To the life with a goal,
To the heart with a hole,
To the throat that is sore,
To the one who sits by the shore,
I will take you to him,
I will take you there,
Where no man sleep,
Where no one's six feet deep,
Where all sit under the tree,
Where the air is set free,
Where all gaze at the stars,
To the place, you can show your scars,
He will tell the story untold,
Get amazed by the secrets as they unfold.

www.ingramcontent.com/pod-product-compliance
Lightning Source LLC
LaVergne TN
LVHW020536160826
845677LV00015B/4086

* 9 7 9 8 7 1 2 0 9 8 4 6 0 *